Snapshots
An On-Growing Collection of Poems (2012-2016)

by Sam Ricky West
aka Samuel (Sa·mwel) Oeste

Dear Readers,

At the genesis of this chapbook, I set out to write poems about things that were actually worth writing about. So I picked up a pen, some napkins, and started jotting words. I opened my eyes, ears, hands, and heart. And after picking up a laptop to compile it all, I found that this, my first book of poems, was about love and loss. I write to capture moments of love as they truly are: broken, fleeting, sinful and painful, yet still beautiful. I write with the resolve that such snapshots matter, for if they do not, what does? I write about stories full of culture & family, privilege & struggle, faith & doubt, power & weakness. Stories that take place in Oakland, DF, UCLA, East San Jose, Linda Vista, and Nicaragua. I write about things and places that have been dynamic in the past year. I write in the USA in a time when it is grappling to understand itself as its culture changes with eagle speed.

My voice comes from growing up in San Diego, and being a college graduate in his twenties. However, I also speak the words of Elena, about being a Norwegian immigrant who served as a Navy nurse for the U.S. in World War II, the words of Jorge about graduating with honors from UCLA and about those deported in his family, and the words of Ryan of being a black male in the days of Oscar, Trayvon, Emmett and so many others. There are words of celebration, joy, and friendship that I long to share. There are also words of pain, judgment, and hurt that I also must embrace. There are words in English and words, occasionally, but unapologetically and unitalicized, in Spanish—for we must embrace all our lenguas. All these voices and countless others from writers, friends, and family blend into my poems. How do they interact, react, and create something new? What ratio of each creates the distinctive flavor of these poems? Now it is your time, as the reader, to taste and imagine for yourself, as well as to see what images, experiences, and lessons it recalls for you. ¡Buen provecho!

1

Book 1: L·oss & Luv

A special thanks to my dear friends who also acted as my Editors: Rebecca Tang, Ariel Waitkuweit, Adam Provinchain, Sara Vetter, and Rojas. I met Rebecca and Ariel in Professor Yenser's poetry writing workshop during our time at UCLA. Beyond his ability to be a master poet matchmaker, I am very grateful for his guidance during that class. I want to give a special shoutout to Ariel who has been helping me edit dilligently until the very last edits. I am grateful for how much fun it is to write with Adam, another UCLA engineering graduate. I am thankful for Sara for years of poetry feedback. May you experience real shalom in your new marriage and journeys ahead. Finally, I am so grateful for the many non-poets like Rojas who keep us tethered to the grit of reality! Of course, there are so many others who have helped me to edit my poetry and have inspired my words. I hope to acknowledge each of you properly in ways you best receive.

Prelude from Lamentations 1

If we lament the violence against people of color in our nation,
perhaps we will not have to lament our own destruction.

She was princess, now
she slaves. Bitterly
she weeps, mourns, finds no
rest. Oh Lord, behold
her affliction, her
grieving, wandering,
and her soul's many
       groans.

Let us suffer, pain,
weep with overflow
of tears, torment, groan
without comfort; oh,
my groans are many,
my heart is. so. faint.

To Rage Against It
For Henri Nouwen, for Noe, for you in this struggle

Clinging to Abel's blood-drenched sheepskin,
Adam raged against it that would also murder me. He raged with the bitter cry of pain.
The hollow days, absent of emotion,
overflow with danger; a heart grows callouses by days and days of rubbing against its grain,

yet no one takes her to the doctor.
Why doesn't she just go take a walk—won't the fresh air make her all better?
As if she hadn't thought of that.
As if his righteous repeat, *love you mija*, should cut through the friction between them,

so he could blame her.
Mom was told that it's genetic, kind of like alcoholism or like breast cancer.
Scrubbing it clean,
she used concentrated bleach to remove the stink and shame of the blood flooded tiles,

still on display like Aaron's golden calf.
A gyroscope would show my wilderness wanderings like an ant running a Mobius strip.
Does Mom hate me?
That I scrub to remove the layers of callouses, from cutting against my heart's grain?

For not wanting another day of this?
Noe had friends, family, but no one could locate the tearing pain in his head,
and no one took him to the doctor.
He thought he was better than them because he had reached the edge, and had not jumped off;

he only replaced rage with madness.
Dad told stories of captured Allied spies who would kill themselves as a last act of free will—
fault implies responsibility implies control.
Like grasping a rocky overhang, tired and scanning for the next hidden hold. I ask,

Not my fault? To hell it isn't! Whose then?
Kiddo, finally let yourself mourn; let yourself rage and yell the beautiful, beautiful cry of pain.
Like Adam's release
of that sheepskin so stained, you can replace madness with rage.

Texts Sent in Grief

For Abuelita, Oliver, Jesus, and Grandpa

from: 8581234567@vtext.com
to: Manny, the temptation is 2hurry,
busy myself 2crowd out the
still moments: like havin
2wait   4   this   lecture   2start.
haha!
I fear them because they brighten up
the scars of my heart, revealin
their weight (u get me?) Instead
of just coverin it up with Spotify,
Im *tryin* 2find it is a dog, ferocious
if u run from it in fear, friendly
if u greet it calmly, head-on.

But how to weigh a heart?
Is it weighed by memories of the
lost? Or by the cares of the future?
Or worries of 2day?
Or doubts? Or pains?
Or merely an accumulation of life's
shit? As a wanderer through the dark
thoughts of worthlessness and suicide,
I know a weighted heart is a workin
heart; a broken heart is a beatin heart.
I fear not the day where these deaths
give me pain: the remorse of a good
bye or bittersweet memories. Im *tryin*
2fight against a calloused heart.
These layers, grown for protection
against pain, also stunt joy. 2scrubbit
clean, dammit!!! 2mourn! Cuz
the heart that can pain, can also joy.

to: Clay, the book says, *it is not*
good for man to be alone. It seems
2have nothin 2do with sex, everything
with luv. Bangin my bed never
helps. 2be fully known; 2fully kno.
U kno? U feel me be4 words slip out,
be4 an explanation, just from a pain
filled quiver. The best romances
find such fellowship, but all fellowships
find such luv. 4us singles, it's the moment
in ur car, spillin Jack In the Box
taco sauce and fry crumbs. We left crumbs
2the way of compassion;
I will be with u,
I will even get in the shit with u.

This is not just a gift from God
but God's very presence,
2my la-ooonly soul.

to: Amiga, after that viewin,
I think I now understand the word cadaver:
a stiff, object-like, lifelessly layin
body, left like a mask from the man.
As if he was replaced with a cold
marble statue. As the statue lies
it can't display the luv, passion,
pain that paint a face and make it
a person. I understand how a
student can dissect a body, assurin
themselves this has ceased 2be someone
or how the faith woman says
the soul has left—reassurin me
that it was never the skin, hair, eyes,
noes, beauty, pride, strength or weakness
that ever kept us alive.

to: God,
Why are U repeatin
death, death, death, death,
4x this year? Be4
she was only a foreigner,
a childhood vapor of a memory
of my mother's tears 4her daughter,
of my father's anger, of my desire
2cry or rage 2, but not bein able
2comprehend their explanations
of why death meant so much.
Her incompressibility
didn't change with familiarity.
Though she steals my heart
like a lover, why is now a moment
of tears? Now a lull? Now anger?
Now confusion?
Perhaps that is inherited from Adam,
holdin Abel's sheepskin,
lookin up, wonderin, askin,
will we ever get back to Eden?

to: Soul,
what did David see at Ziklag
when u seemed so silent?
Where did Mandela find peace
in a cell of fear and hate?
Would I find it if I could
hear the voice commandin
breathe BREATHE breathe,
beat BEAT beat?

Queries for The Mother

Inspired by El Sueño De La Malinche
Oh, what do you dream of Doña Marina?
Do you dream of a white cathedral
perched on your hill, sitting like the conquest,
like the one you tunnel to day by day?
As you dream on your bed of brass
under golden sheets, on two feather pillows,
do you see Cortés, the first man to see your
wisdom without fear, your will without disdain,
your talents with much greed and asked,
Do the riches of the Aztecs please you?

Oh, what do you dream of Malinalli?
Do you still dream of a Mayan home
housing a king, now with grayed hair,
who failed to also be father
and of the queen whispering schemes sitting
to his left, supporting his muscled arm?
When you dream of the moment that you
smell the flowers of home again are you
dressed again in a grass skirt and a princess'
jewels, or are you riding, supporting the arm
of Cortés, as a conqueror?

Oh, of what do you nightmare, La Malinche?
Do you fear for Martín now away from you
in the world you have created for him,
in the world split by the valleys of war,
where natives now hide among anciet hills
or make their last stand on the mountains,
as you mediate between rulers of old
and the new that will now never leave?
Do you hold your head for your children
whom rest on the foundations of your body,
who will call you traitor and *la chingada,*
who will fear you, who will see you with greed,
who will distain you as you lay forever under
the weight of the world that sold you into slavery
then blamed you for the choices that you made
to survive, to claim your own path, to mother
a new people that you carried in your womb
and who will fall to the underworld if you
were you to ever to rise up to free yourself
from your dream?

San Jose Starbucks Napkin 4
for Dora

Who picked this picture
of coffee trees?
(¿muy idílica, no?)
The woman stands tall,
with a plain brown dress,
blue umbrella and white shawl,
unstained, unworn.
It is not a fit for work;
It is not raining or even
so sunny. Tell me
the truth, who picked
this coffee?

Mi Cuarta Servilleta en Starbucks
para Dora

¿Quién es la mujer
en este foto, Starbucks,
(¿muy idílica, no?)
con su paragua sin
llover, vestido largo
y café sin desgaste
y con una espalda
alta y orgullosa,
como el Madroño?
¿Quién, Starbucks,
cogió este café?

The Heat of the Melting Pot
Whichever of you is without sin, throw
the first stone (John 8:7)

How we looked them down, lined up
next to fifty pound gravel bags
at the Home Depot's
façade. The cruelest jokes
receive the loudest laughs.

How the gray with his Ford-f150 there for gardening
supplies looked them down, their brown skin
signifying *economic opportunity*. Across the shopping
center, Vons employees carry white
posters to demand benefits and wage increases.
We've left burns from the heat of *The Melting Pot*.

Was this stone wall between us born in
our high school Mexican jokes when he laughed too;
we didn't know, tio Gerardo makes an annual migration
as one of millions of seasonal workers who still harvest
our crop of California's Citrus Belt.
Yet they hold no share in our *The Land of Opportunity*.

I am white—but I call Jorge *my hermano*
although *my uncles* are not separated by a barbed wire fence
by the Sonora Desert with her hidden water bottles. They
are slashed if found. *Run fast Jorge, La Migra is coming.*

Tio Ernesto is a 52-year-old father-of-five, raising his family
in California, deported this year for his *crime*—
illegal entry when he was 2.

Call this poem what you want: *appeasement,*
democrat mumbo jumbo,
just remember it happens;
and *my people* will not read this poem.

Love Ye Therefore the Stranger
Inspired by Desert Blood

The brown Lincoln
dropped at a Jack-in-the-Box
drive-thru window will never
be picked up. *A penny saved*
is a penny earned.

There have been hundreds of border workers murdered
in the past 20 years. Femicides are much more common
in Juarez than any city in the U.S. or in Mexico.
Yet for the love of GDP, for the U.S. production
of new silver dimes, the maquiladoras
run on unconcerned. *O Love*
is the crooked thing.

Clinton signed the NAFTA agreement,
allowing brown labor to pay Bill's
spending plans and they are paying him
in pennies for his thoughts.
A new maquiladoras plant
is opening today melting down forgotten coppers
to make America's shining white BMWs,
for quixotic knights to ride in. *Nothing new*
is under the sun.

Maquiladoras are vultures
searching for mujeres del sur
for their dark skin,
for *economic opportunity,*
to offer border traders
waiting for a new cheap labor shipment,
The American Dream has always run on that power.
Lest it is thought that exploitative American labor
ended with Abe.

Ah, penny, brown penny,
brown brown brown
beautiful.
brown. penny.
Why have we not loved you?

Dios Da

while praying for Baltimore.
I hid under the dangling branches
of the Deodar.

Its rough calloused bark,
covered by spotty
moss,
supported my droopy
head. Ensename a sostener
otras con esta fuerza.

God gave us the spring jacaranda:
a beautiful mezcla of

green   and   yellow
shimmering leaves   and   wrinkling seed pods
Danos esta habilidad de vivir en armonía.

13

Part 1: Fruitvale Station

You want me selling dope bruh? □
I got a family, got a girl to marry, □
got a daughter. What do you want from me? □□

He was a marked man, jailed,
□institutionalized, scorned,
□rejected, a man of sorrows,

□□murdered like a stray. □He
promised T, *Imma be fine.* □
His fault for lying? Whose fault□
for his dying? Blood on hands.□□

What is life but chances?
Odds? □Starting near the finish
or so behind?□□

Peter white
rich
criminal□
heart
slowly beat beat
□beating
□asleep□□

Oscar black
poor
□criminal□
heart
slowly bleed bleed□
bleeding□
asleep□□

America, you fucking used me
like a joint you smoked
to a nub, flicked to concrete, □
crushed with □*your converses.* □□

God, forgive us, for□
we have killed your sons.□

Part 2: I Started to write *If They Gunned Me Down,*
empathizing with the loss,
showing we all lose when life's lost,
struggling to imagine the grief and pain,
fighting with thousands for justice to gain,
but I stopped.
I cannot, will not, should not
read rhetoric but not face reality.
I reject the easy way out.
Because of my skin, I would not have been
Michael Brown but Gunman White.
If I gunned him down,
I would be protected
from incriminating pictures in the news.
from weeping for my son,
from worrying for my nephews,
from protest for my justice,
from being killed,
And I would be *innocent.*
Though I did not gun him down,
I'm ashamed of him that did.
I apologize, God please forgive,
God make justice here live.

I write to not ignore but explore
a story that is not mine
but a history that is.
I write because ignorance
is the ill-used privilege
of my race that I reject.
Michael could not choose to ignore,
so neither do I. To say nothing
is to take a side, is to gun him down.
As long as the black dead
fall on the streets from Missouri
to L.A., I have to say,
No unarmed American
should be shot to death.
God.
Make justice here live.

Part 3: My Tweet on #Black Lives Matter
So we gather
Even use twitter
Protest rather
than accept the matter
As our ass is on the line
cuz injustice anywhere *is* always mine.

15

Part 1: I Remember Abuelita

An Eulogy for Elena Opager Reifel, 1920-2013

I don't remember hello,
but I remember
her goodbye,
and one left unsaid.

I remember her last words to me,
I love you. I remember the knot
tightening the threads of my stomach
and wondering if it was the last one.
I remember fantically calling,
searching for an earlier ride home.
Abuelita I will miss you so much.

I remember wishing for a blessing
though I already had two blankets,
each seam held together by love:
by her wrinkled fingers, by her focused eyes,
by her back bent. I remember wanting to hear her stories,
writing them down as my first biography.
I remember that it was the first time I thought,
so this is where I come from.

I remember Spanish Scrabble.
Though she was too old to understand the rules;
we made our own. She recited, *Ohhh!*
Beba agua, that means drink water!
and waited for me to play it. It Almost like she
was still in Panama, as if she was still a Navy nurse,
as if I was an old friend as well as a grandchild.
I scrapped the idea of turns and just filled
the board with her words—both of us winners.

I remember Sherlock Holmes in black and white.
Sometimes she cried, *Oh wow! That was quite an ending.*
But sometimes she just fell asleep cuz
we had seen that one too many times.
I remember it being our time no matter
what else was going on. I remember kissing her forehead,
saying, *I love you abuelita, goodbye.*

I remember her calling Robert a bum—the worst
thing she ever called anyone. I remember that moment
I realized that I am my grandma's and my own.

I remember that her blanket had the power
to help me sleep in the tiny Dykstra Hall dorm
despite the weed that permiated everything
and despite the bass from the party next door.

I remember her stories of nursing school
and how much she loved to learn.
The wonderful opportunity of education.
I remember driving her to Sew Hut
and her many gray, gay friends.

I remember the days of heavy breathing,
with no more appetite, with not knowing
tomorrow would come, and still she smiled at me.
I remember running to catch up to her as she
took her morning, trying to absorb her love, her life,
her personality. I remember the day she climbed
the lemon tree her strong legs, like frail frayed rope,
still able. Just not to come down. I remember her
falls and her black-red-blue bruises. I remember
that she posed for a photo-op, bandages on her head, rips on her arm—
how it became an icon for us grandkids. My oldest brother
showing it to his fiancé, saying, *Isn't she awesome?*

I remember asking her what Norwegian people
ate for Christmas—her answer was *Lutefisk*;
I googled it later just to make sure.
I remember coming home my last night,
her asleep on the coach—waiting until midnight
to make sure she got to say goodbye before I left to UCLA.
Somehow, she knew.

My grandma passed away 5:20 this morning. It is 10:51 am.
Already it is not what I remember that bothers me, but that
which I don't. What if I forget how her arms feel
when she clung to me in a hug? Or how her eyes dance
as she sewed or rearranged her room? Or how she hurries
ahead to meet her daughter Claire? Or runs to the phone
to answer Cathy? Or her strong 92-year-old arms that hold
her great-grand-children Luke and Caleb. Or that weak hand
 that need help opening water bottles? Or her darkening eyes?
Or when she learned brail? Or learned Spanish?
Or to perform surgery? Or to Facebook?
Or to sew? Or to paint? Or to sail? Or to dance? Or to love?
Or when first learn the feel of her mother's hand?
Or when she clinged onto my mother's with her last breath?

17

Part 2: Hello until goodbye; goodbye until hello.

I write to not forget,
cuz I sometimes forget that I write
to have something more than two blankets,
a black-and-white Holmes movie,
su español y su fe,
her sense of adventure, and eagerness
to climb a tree, even if I
too need to be carried home.

Grandma Tree by the Roadside

Her back wrinkled, striped, hardened,
strong by rain, sun, wind,
rain, sun.

Her branches, twisted towards a parked
Sedan, are wise to avoid the shadows
cast by bricks.

Her roots roamed rich soils
shrewd, discerning nutrients from gravel, water, clay,
decomposing mass.

Her leaves adorned her days
sensible to the season, coloring them avacado green,
chile yellow, cayenne red, bean brown.

Guíame en los caminos de vidas ricas;
Protégeme bajo la sombra de tus alas.

3 AM Phone Call
Inspired by Tattoos on the Heart

Hi G, I have a question....
Have I been your son?

I hear his voice waver and falter.
Cesar longed not just for a father,
rather to be a son worth having.
Through his terrors,
histories of hurt,
through his wilderness wanderings,
He yearned to hear
a father, claim him as,

be-luv-ed son,

Rest in being lovingly chosen,
well pleasing, this name I call you
is cemented on heaven's streets.

Summer Art Camp
for Maria

Swinging herself through a two bar- wide hole in the chipped-white-wrought-iron -fence,
 which is a goal
for the boy's spontaneous soccer games that leave bare scars across the lawn, she
 stumbles, but regains
her usual four-year-old -half-skip-half-walk. I eye my black pilot pen and my
 half-finished lesson plan
scribbled across a yellow pad, and after a limbo -moment, I resign. I set it
 on the freshly blue painted table
signed with the painters' twenty red and white handprints: their Fourth of July's
 mess-of-kids-painting.
She sneaks behind me and greets me with *BOO! Sam, lets go play in the back,*
 tugging my hand.
I was surprised, not that she wanted me to take her to the newly fixed swing set but by
 how early she was today—
probably to escape out of the too-small -apartment, or to arrive before bullying brothers
 shove her off the swing set.
She remembers everything, especially how high Manuel and Gerry can swing, exclaiming
 push me lika-Gerry;
push me to outer-space! I remind her necesitas decir por favor, and we begin to chat
 Spanish, English, and Spanglish
about her family's new baby on the way. Later, she will play cook. Instructions: *Mix together*
 sand, rocks, and ice
plant leaves, then call *Sam! eat mis pupusas for you,* because baby-stop-pretending
 is Manuel's response.
But, for now, she can fly high, kicking the top of the shed's concrete wall as satisfied as if
 it really were the moon.

Like the Hunted Deer in a Clearing
Inspired by "Like Land Crabs"

walking warily
with weighed feet
clinging to pavement patches,

we eat *TAMALES! TAMALES Y CHAMPURRADO!*
with spicy smells so inviting we
burn our tongues, wanting to fit in
wanting our white skin

to not stand out. But, colorblind is a myth.
My epidermis is not concealable
like a gazelle in the swaying savanna.

Should we wave to the porch sitters
with wise worldly eyes? We walk
on, as if the blotchy cement
was an undiscovered substance
we had not yet determined

to be safe.

What Is Ignored
for Esteban

Pale morning lightly kisses
the not-yet warm pavement
sliding under thin legs
of a skirted girl with her blue
and gold jacket protecting her

from the wind, honest to the season
it coolly blows off her hood
and hair about her face. She takes
little notice, inserting in earbuds
as her legs propel her anxiously

onward. A red-paint speckled
golden leaf, wind-detached, once
green. Now its search for rest
ends preemptively as it glides
onto her shoulder. She brushes

it off. The white chalk
chatters, sometimes squealing
for empathy, and she will take
copious notes on biology, her hand
now on the heavy wooden
lecture hall door, but she pauses
until she can squeeze in. Below, ants
swarm up through pavement cracks.

The Return to Our Rendezvous
for Hermanita

Students shall swarm
Shall swarm in
Swarm inside
Side of coffee
Of coffee house
Coffee house quick
House quick fix
Quick fix for
Fix for times
For time's ticks
Time's ticks that
Ticks that trick
That trick away
Trick away Netflix's
Away Netflix's day
Netflix's day study
Day study stress
Study stress sweet
Stressed sweet Student
Sweet Student bee
Student bee just
Be just be.

Savor the Sweet Bites
For My Ex

It was buried under calculus textbooks, lying
tangent to your words, writ' two days before
twelve times we circled, that house lost in thoughts
of us, four weeks before you declared *I love
you*, (But did you?) when only two weeks later
you and he lay under Orion's watchful
eyes and I only forgave you months later
during the days of your academic probation,
the days your father took us for Bulgogi
to feed me, feed him, feed you, with questioning
eyes, months before unanswered calls, before
I can't do this texts, before we sat savoring
last bites of frosted vanilla strawberry cake.
It would end up stale, growing only mold.
The days of, *Are you fucking anyone yet?*
And *Sam, I'm calling to say I'm sorry
And goodbye*. Now I white-knuckle grip onto
your paper-thin words. Do I hold the truth
hiding behind eyes, these months where space between
us was measured in astronomical units,
or was it that confession, soon forgotten,
or this fading phantom revived for a moment
(kiddo, such memories, not words, are this
moment's truth) to replace a yellowing card?

Chick-Fil-A Mesas
For Remmy

A blond pair snack down chicken with
    smacking lips,
    matching caps,
    touching hips.

A frayed gray wears a cross cross her
    holy breasts
    between her
    and the rest.

A brown face hidden under a cap
    only hears
    iPod buds
    in his ears.

A bald head named *Guest* on his heavy chest
    habla de casa,
    trabajo,
    la raza.
    El gringo
    ofrece
    sus manos
    a *mija,*
    bajo del
    escudo,
    la mesa.

A half white named *Nate* takes trays
    Would you sit
    over there
    novia?
    Or would we
    let lips smack,
    let caps match,
    let hips touch?
    My table
    he wipes clean,
    maybe fresh.

Thank you.
Sincerely, Sam.

www.ingramcontent.com/pod-product-compliance
Lightning Source LLC
Chambersburg PA
CBHW080553030426
42337CB00024B/4864